THE TIME OF YOUR LIFE

The Time

POEMS

Of

J. R. SOLONCHE

Your Life

Adelaide Books
New York / Lisbon
2020

THE TIME OF YOUR LIFE
a collection of poems by
J.R. Solonche

Copyright © 2020 by J.R. Solonche
Cover design: Adelaide Books LLC

Published by Adelaide Books, New York / Lisbon
adelaidebooks.org

Editor-in-Chief
Stevan V. Nikolic

All rights reserved. No part of this book may be reproduced in any manner whatsoever without written permission from the author except in the case of brief quotations embodied in critical articles and reviews.

For any information, please address Adelaide Books
at info@adelaidebooks.org
or write to:
Adelaide Books LLC
244 Fifth Ave. Suite D27
New York, NY, 10001

ISBN: 978-1-952570-27-8

Printed in the United States of America

Contents

The Time of Your Life *9*
I Was Out of Place There *10*
I Went for a Walk *11*
Outside *12*
That Was Another Time *13*
There's Not Much Left to Say *14*
Imagined or Imagined *15*
Uncle Poetry *16*
Purple *17*
April *18*
Of Course *20*
I Bought Them *21*
On a Picture Entitled Jesus at Twelve Years of Age *22*
Colonoscopy *23*
Finding a Flower Pressed Between Pages of the
1887 Edition of *The Early Poems of John Greenleaf Whittier* *24*
Nighthawks by Edward Hopper *26*
The Mink *27*
Saturday Morning *28*
Crimson Cyclamen *29*
At Dusk I Am as Tired as the World *33*
The Trees *34*
The First Seven Steps of the Buddha-to-Be *35*

To a Student Who Lied about the Trees in a Poem Called *Autumn* 36
Two Hours of Reading 37
Funeral Oration for Alan Dugan 38
The Half Not Heard 39
Second Warning to a Young Poet 40
Moving In 41
The Simple Past 44
What the Dead Said 45
The Poet from Nepal 46
Dog Ghazal 47
Undo 48
Because Understanding Ends It Does Not Mean All Ends 49
I Don't Believe You Don't Remember 50
Masturbation 51
Autumn 52
My Lilac Is Dying 53
Coltsfoot 54
The Peacock 55
Metamorphosis 56
You Should Just Let It Go 57
On the Passing of Philip Roth 58
Nine Yellow Lilies 59
The Melancholy of Anatomy 60
The Fun of Poetry 61
Van Gogh 62
Stargazer Lilies 63
When I Get Up 64
To Each Her Own 65
Four Short Rosebush Poems 66
Brown Freckles 68

The Only Thing   *69*
Attraction   *70*
A Piece of Real Estate   *71*
On the Passing of Clarence Fountain   *73*
I Have No Use for the Phrases   *74*
Reassurance   *75*
Poem Beginning with a Line from an Old Chinese Poem   *76*
The Breeze   *77*
Flowers of Guilt   *78*
If Days Like This Rare Day   *79*
Every Place Must   *80*
O, Happy Hour   *81*
Over the Clouds   *82*
Wild Cherry Tree in August   *83*
Red Vinca   *84*
The Shadows that Shadow Me   *85*
The Old Rosebush   *87*
The Mushrooms   *88*
The Acorns   *89*
The Hummingbird at the Empty Feeder   *90*
Metaphor   *91*
The Next Time   *92*
The Nowhere   *93*
Petunias   *94*
I Am Waiting for Something   *95*
Summer   *96*
One Is Forced to Admire It   *97*
In the Depth at the Height of Summer   *98*
The Music   *99*

Acknowledgments   101
About the Author   103

The Time of Your life

That was when there was time.
That lasted a long time.

Then life happened.
That lasted a short time.

Then life said, "It's your turn."
Time said, "Whatever, it's your life."

They were twins separated before birth.
They were together in passing.

They passed for each other.
They passed like ships in the night.

One winked.
The other waved.

J.R. Solonche

I Was Out of Place There

I was out of place there.
It was no place to be.

There was no place else to go.
There was no home-like place.

I hated hats.
I hated the fedora with the feather.

I hated the cab driver's cap.
I hated anything on my head.

I hated the skullcap.
I hated the hand.

I was the one who saw the butterfly.
I was the one who saw the omelet.

I was the one who did not see the blood.
I was the one who passed the test.

"We are the One, and they are the Zero," he said.
He was going fishing.

There was a marlin on the wall.
For a moment, I wished I had been one.

I envied his wild eye, and I envied his weapon.
One of us was out of place there.

I Went for a Walk

It was after breakfast.
"Good morning,"
the earth said to me.
"How are you?"
"I'm well," I said.
"How are you?"
"Oh, I'm tired."
"Tired?" I said.
"Yes, tired," said
the earth. "Tired,
oh, so tired of being
the world."

Outside

The rain stops,
the sun comes out,
and for the first time in my life,
I have gotten a hard-on for a fucking flower.

THE TIME OF YOUR LIFE

That Was Another Time

That was another time.
It was a long time ago.

It was yesterday.
It was a long time ago.

I remember it as if it were yesterday.
You were there.

You looked exactly the same.
You hadn't aged a bit.

That was a different time.
It was a long time ago.

It was tomorrow.
You weren't there.

I was by myself.
I was the same as always.

I hadn't changed a bit.
I was not myself.

Neither was I anyone else.
It was another place.

It should have been strange.
But it wasn't.

There's Not Much Left to Say

There's not much left to say.
I must say so much more in order to say it right.

Someone must stop me when I've done it.
I don't know who it should be.

I know who it will be.
It will be you.

Unlike the others, do not burn it all.
Burn only the excess.

That will be almost all.
Do not let it go on too long.

Burn what goes on too long.
Get my attention.

Get me to stop.
Kill me.

Kill what is left of me.
It will not be much.

Imagined or Imagined

It was real only when it was real.
It was imagined forever thereafter.

The difference disappeared in real time.
It disappeared while it was happening before my eyes.

The difference was a smell.
The difference was a taste.

The difference was one tear wide.
The difference felt different.

The difference was lighter.
The difference dissolved on my tongue.

It became its next word.
It made no difference what the word was.

Nothing was left to the imagination.
Imagine my surprise.

J.R. Solonche

Uncle Poetry

I've never been an uncle.
I never had a nephew or a niece.
It would be nice.
I have a brother, but he never had children.
An uncle is just another thing I'll never be,
unless you out there can be my nephews and nieces.
Then you can call me "Uncle Poetry."

Purple

Everyone looks good in it.
Everything looks wonderful in it.
The sky looks good in purple.
The purple marten looks wonderful in it.
The emperors and empresses,
regardless of their cruelty,
looked good, looked wonderful in purple.

April

Looking in the mirror this morning
while I was shaving,
I paused with the electric razor on my cheek,
the razor still gnashing the cheek-skin,
and I asked myself, "Solonche, are you supposed
to see anything in the mirror besides your face?"
Then that question led to another question,
which was, "Solonche, is the mirror
supposed to be a window or a door?"
Then that question led to another question,
which was, "Solonche, are you supposed to see
your father through the window
or through the door the mirror
is supposed to be, and is your father sitting
at the kitchen table, silently threatening to die?"
Then that question led to another question,
which was, "Solonche, are you supposed to see
yourself as a boy through the window or the door,
the boy you were many years ago, sitting at
the kitchen table, silently threatening to live?"
Then that question led to another,
which was, "Solonche, are you now supposed
to see yourself as an old man many but not many
years from now, silently threatening to die?"
Then that question led to, "Solonche,
are you supposed to see yourself as dead,
no longer anyone, but only the cheek-bone

beneath the cheek-skin beneath the cheek-stubble
you are shaving?" Then that question led
to no other questions, for there were no others,
so I finished shaving without answering
these questions, and I went out
this fine, first week of April morning
and I saw, there on the front lawn,
the wild cherry tree,
and the wild cherry tree was in full bloom,
the wild cherry tree was a cumulus cloud
of white cherry blossoms,
the wild cherry tree was half the sky and half
the earth, and an answer bloomed,
an answer like a white cumulus cloud
filled half of my mind, and the answer was,
"Yes, the wild cherry tree in full bloom!"
and another answer bloomed like a white
cumulus cloud and filled half of my mind,
and it was, "No, the wild cherry tree in full bloom!"

Of Course

Of course, I understand you must protect yourself.
Of course, I understand you have been hurt.

Of course, I understand your heart is tender.
Of course, I understand one father is enough.

Of course, I understand there is no future here.
Of course, I understand it is best this way.

Of course, I understand it is impossible.
Of course, I understand that it's understood.

Of course, I understand that it's all my fault.
Of course, I understand that I am to blame.

Of course, I understand that "things happen."
Of course, I understand this way is best.

Of course, I understand that apologies can be lies.
Of course, I understand.

I Bought Them

I bought them,
two big books,
fat with two lifetimes of poems,

not so much to read them,
which, over a long time, as is meant, I will do,
but just to look at,

their bigness,
heavy as loaves of grainy peasant bread,
and their pictures on the covers,

the two old Polish poets,
Milosz and Herbert,
their beautiful white hair,

their beautiful long white fingers,
their beautiful white cigarettes,
and the smoke like their own beautiful white ghosts.

J.R. Solonche

On a Picture Entitled Jesus at Twelve Years of Age

We have all known such boys
in sixth grade. Tall, slim, athletically
built but not an athlete, serious but not
a great reader nor the scientific sort,
the matinee idol profile that drives
the giggly girls, in whom he shows
no interest, crazy (even the high school
girls have a crush on him), yet something
tender, perhaps effeminate about the corners
of the mouth, the cherubic lips, the eyes' long lashes,
the poet who doesn't write poetry but only looks
as though he did, the odd one the other kids
have given up teasing, the loner who has no friends,
who lingers on the edges of things, even in class,
sitting by the window where he can look out
of this world altogether, look out at the crystalline
blue of sky and the clouds, white as shrouds,
and then turn toward his teacher (she too
is secretly in love with him) with an expression
she has seen before only on the faces of runaways.

Colonoscopy

The idiotic nurse wanted
to give me an extra set of pictures
to take home. What sort
of patient did she take me for?
What did she expect me to do
with pictures of my colon?
Carry them around in my wallet?
Put them in silver frames on
my desk next to my wife
and daughter? *Keep them,* I said.
You don't want them? she said.
Nope, throw 'em out, I said.
She looked insulted. I felt bad.
I should have taken them.
Dear nurse, I apologize.
Please do not curse my eyes.

J.R. Solonche

Finding a Flower Pressed Between Pages of the 1887 Edition of *The Early Poems of John Greenleaf Whittier*

There is no point in wondering who put it here,
or why, although such wandering
might make some pressing poetry.

There is no message here, no mystery in this flower
for curiosity to open up or code to break.
Judging from the size and shape, it is perhaps a lily.

There is no color anymore.
A lily. Perfect if it is a lily.
Perfect if it is a lily in a book of verse.

Some sentimentalist put a lily in this book,
in the poem "The Bridal of Pennacook."
Perhaps it was a little girl.

THE TIME OF YOUR LIFE

But no. It must have been a bride.
A bride must have put this lily here.
A bride left this lily here, and what is left of her

is less than this, and what is known of her
is only this: This part of the paper,
this part of the poem, this once a flower,

once a lily, this lily's ghost, this dry and brittle, at most
like a brown leaf in the book *The Early Poems of Greenleaf,*
in the poem "The Bridal of Pennacook."

J.R. Solonche

Nighthawks by Edward Hopper

I don't wonder about them really,
the four in the coffee shop,
the nighthawks (if you count
the short-order cook as a nighthawk),
the man with his back to us, absorbed
in his own thoughts, or listening
to the conversation between the couple
and the short-order cook. I wonder
about the family up there in that
apartment above their own restaurant
across the street, in bed on this hot
summer night with the windows open.
I wonder about the wife, who is
sobbing silently to herself, thinking
about the boyfriend who jilted her
back in high school because the man
with his back to us reminds her of him.
I wonder about the husband, who is
smiling silently to himself because he
is having a wet dream about the redhead.
I wonder about the teenaged daughter,
who is now, in minute detail,
planning her escape.

The Mink

It was the mink.
It was the mink with the glass bead eyes
and the satin lining that hung on the inside
of my mother's closet door.
It was the mink
with the glass bead eyes and the satin lining
that confused me so.
It was how I did not know
why death should smell of fresh flowers,
why death could have such eyes
that confused me so.
It was for the rest of my life.

J.R. Solonche

Saturday Morning

"So tell me, what will happen to me
when I die, when I take my last breath?"
I asked the Jehovah's Witness who came
to my door. "Oh, you'll fall into a deep
deep sleep, "she said. "And then you'll wake
up, and guess what, you'll be young again."
"So okay, I'll be resurrected. And how old
will I be when I wake up?" "Twenty," she said.
I frowned. "But I don't want to be twenty.
I didn't like being twenty when I was twenty
the first time. Could I be thirty?" "Oh, yeah,
okay, you can be thirty." "And will there be
beer there in heaven?" "Oh, sure, guess what,
any kind of beer you want." "Really? Samuel
Smith's Tadcaster Oatmeal Stout?" She nodded.
"This is great," I said. "Could I get this in writing?"
"Well, no," she said. "You mean I only have your
word for it?" She nodded. "Too bad," I said.
"Listen, go back to your Kingdom Hall and
see if you can get that in writing, that I'll be thirty
and have all the Samuel Smith's Tadcaster
Oatmeal Stout I want for all eternity. I'll do
anything else Jehovah wants, sing, play the harp,
witness…" "Bye now, have a nice day," she said,
a twinkle in her eye. Too bad. Too damn bad.

Crimson Cyclamen

See The Collected Poems of William Carlos Williams Vol. I 1909 – 1939
Ed. A. Walton Litz and Christopher MacGowan
(New Directions,1986)

Hardcover	21 used from $8.86
		18 new from $42.71
Paperback	91 used from $6.06
		52 new from $18.84
Kindle Edition $14.99

"W. C. Williams's poems are about as important to modern American poetry as the Rocky Mountains are to the American continent: you can't get around them. As the reviews here indicate, he's still not to everyone's taste, but his influence is enormous, largely defining great areas of subsequent American verse (most of which however in my opinion isn't nearly as good as Williams himself.) If you are at all seriously interested in modern American poetry, you should have this collection in your library."
4 people found this helpful

"I bought this book for my husband for his birthday and he absolutely loves it. This is a very comprehensive copy of William Carlos Williams works and has intelligent and thoughtful footnotes."
2 people found this helpful

"I had to write something similar on Volume II--just typing to fill the word count. This is William Carlos Williams. That's it."
One person found this helpful

"Shipped quickly, as described...."
One person found this helpful

"For those that love the Wheelbarrow and Rainwater poem, I believe that is something to be had in this. It may be hard to find, amongst all the others. I came away from this book thinking that he was evolving to fit an emerging pattern of cellphones, mass-media, and multi-media, caught in a past age, while attempting to collect his thoughts about a future that meant something to him. The poems are not futuristic, but they have insight about the future. The poems are tangible and intelligent at the same time. I would not call W C Williams an abstract poet (which is my preference. Most other poets deride the concept that a poet could be abstract in the first place). If you came on the scene expecting the W.C. Williams would be the next Dickinson, you will be sorely disappointed. But every poet has a unique voice."
2 people found this helpful

"I bought this volume and volume 2. Carlos William Carlos was definitely ahead of his time. But I can say except for The Red Wheelbarrow and a few other poems, that he was a radical. I can't say I'm a big fan. Some of the poems were awful the others were just weird!"
One person found this helpful

"Whew, check out that list. This is the foundation of Williams' art, for fans of his selected & Pictures from Brughel. This is the development of Williams' daily art, fine poems punctuated by an occasional masterpiece or near-surrealistic gemstone. Someone once

asked John Cage, "With your methods, couldn't anyone compose music?" Cage replied, "Yes, but they don't." Many of Williams' poems make that impression. Where I live, in New Jersey, Williams is so ingrained in the literary landscape that no poet is more imitated, even if the imitator is unaware of the influence. Williams was better at setting examples than at explaining methods. He learned & invented as he wrote, & I suspect his talk & his letters had a great deal more influence than his occasional stabs at poetics. Williams stripped down American poesy & reconstructed it as a form of talk, which it had been all along beneath Whitman's yawping & Dickinson's obsessive editing & Frost hiking though New England snow five steps at a time. Like all great American originals, he didn't know he was supposed to be a somebody-else; maybe a Stephen Benet, a William Vaughn Moody, an Edwin Arlington Robinson, all big literary stars in their time but not now counted in the first ranks of our poets. This is roughly the first half of The Doc's amazin' journey. You'll know if you need it. Any intelligent poet friend will love it as a gift."
21 people found this helpful

"The overall strength of Williams' work lies in his power to summon image from where there was previously nothing. Forget about the conventional tactics of poetry (meter, rhyme, etc.). Williams effectively occupies the outer regions of the land which is not prose. His power always properly lay in the simple yet vivid images (visual, aural, tactile, etc.) behind the words."
16 people found this helpful

"I'm not going to attempt to talk about WCW's poetry or I could be writing for hours... rather this review is about the volume of "collected" poems as a book to read. Yes it includes some dubious items and some debris we would expect from any serious and innovative writer... but there are mostly successes here and well worth

reading. Especially informative is observing WCW's development as a writer and thinker and his daring as a poet and his striving for new ways to express the response of an artist to the swelling tide of modernity and cultural failures of the 20th century."
7 people found this helpful

At Dusk I Am as Tired as the World

At dusk, I am as tired as the world.
The mind has other dreams to do.

The mind wants to sit in a tree, to wait for the owls.
When the owls wake up to talk to one another, I blush.

I eavesdrop on them and am ashamed.
The mind has to make up its own dreams.

When the dreams make up their minds, I sleep soundly.
When I awake, there is so much unfinished business.

The morning is always as surprised as I am.
The morning always has something more to say.

The mind is never satisfied to let dreams speak for it.
The mind insists upon its own originality.

It doesn't know which side its bread is buttered on.
The mind knows what's good for it, but not what's better.

J.R. Solonche

The Trees

The trees are supposed to be green,
but they are not. It is this fog,
it is this cloud afraid of heights,
that hugs the ground instead,
that embraces also the trees
and has stolen their green.
What does it want with it?
What does this fog want with the color of the trees?
Nothing. It has swallowed their green out of jealousy,
having none of its own.
You know why.
At least you should.
Think of the last time you were jealous.
Think of the last time having none of your own.

The First Seven Steps of the Buddha-to-Be

In the Qing dynasty bronze,
the First Seven Steps of the Buddha-to-be,
the Buddha-to-be has completed the seventh step.
He is standing motionless squarely on both feet.
He is pointing down with the index finger of his right hand.
He is pointing up with the index finger of his left hand.
He is saying, *I need go no farther. This is the way.*
Here is the place between earth and heaven.
So with his eighth step, the Buddha-to-be
will stop counting steps forever.

J.R. Solonche

To a Student Who Lied about the Trees in a Poem Called *Autumn*

Listen, please do not lie about the trees.
Do not say that in autumn all the trees die.

This isn't true.
In autumn, all the leaves die, not the trees.

Some trees die in autumn, just as some trees die in summer,
and some in spring, and some in winter.

But in autumn, what all the trees do is go to sleep.
Autumn is their night, as spring is their morning.

Trees tell time differently from us, you see.
To them, a year is a day.

They go to sleep in autumn and wake up in spring,
just as we go to sleep tonight and wake up tomorrow morning.

So next time you write a poem about autumn,
or about anything else for that matter, please tell the truth.

If you want to lie, because after all, it is a poem that you write,
lie about yourself. Okay?

Two Hours of Reading

Enough. The words
have had enough.
They are dizzy from
their dancing. They
fall asleep before
they hit the floor. I,
too, have had enough.
I close the book with
my left hand. I close
the light with my right.
My eyes close themselves.
My hands? They like
the silence. They like
the dark. They stay
open. Besides, there
is nothing to close them
with. They are all
I have to show for it.
Two hours of reading.

J.R. Solonche

Funeral Oration for Alan Dugan

First of all, this is not a funeral
oration. I didn't attend your funeral.
I wasn't invited. Why should I be?
I'm not family, not even distantly.
I'm not a friend. I'm not an acquaintance.
All I am is a reader. And you don't know
me from Adam. But I thought I would
write this just the same. After all, the
mouse you wrote a funeral oration for
didn't know you from Adam. Okay, so
you were never big enough to make
the cover of *Time,* (Has any poet ever
been big enough to make the cover of *Time?*)
your obit is in it, along with the obits
of Gisele Mackenzie, 76, of colon cancer,
Burbank Calif. and Charles Bronson, 81,
of pneumonia, Los Angeles, and Rand
Brooks, 84, it doesn't say of what, Santa
Ynez, Calif. (Never heard of him either,
actor, played Scarlett O'Hara's first husband
in *Gone With the Wind.*) And you, "Alan
Dugan, 80, American poet who alternately
endeared and offended readers with his
language – with its liberal scatological
references – and such prosaic themes as
drinking, irksome jobs and masturbation,
of pneumonia, in Hyannis, Mass." As if
there were any other way one could endear
or offend. O, American poet.

The Half Not Heard

You said, "I was right."
You said, "I was a nice person."
You said, "Yes, but you have a wife to fall back on."
You said, "Don't you remember the childhood?"
You said, "Don't be surprised if I never see you again."
You said, "Don't you remember?"
You said, "Don't be surprised."

J.R. Solonche

Second Warning to a Young Poet

When you read the words of others that are better than your words,
and that you know in your mind of minds, are better,
you will know jealousy, envy and spite.
They will churn in the pit of your stomach,
and you will want to bring up jealousy, envy and spite
like phlegm and spit jealousy, envy and spite
into the faces of everyone you meet.
You will want to stop your own words from coming.
You will want to bury yourself in the earth.
You will want to crawl on your belly on the ground
and crawl into a dark fissure deep in the earth.
You will want to jump into the sea, from the stern of a ship, in the fog.
You will want to shave your head down to skin.
You will want to rend your favorite blue shirt.
You will want to cut off your right thumb.
You will want to drink cheap red wine until it gurgles back up into your throat.
You will want to curse the moon when it is full and when it is gone.
You will write the first of many poems about writing your last poem.
You will want to be martyred, shot through and through with pens.
You will want to take up golf.

THE TIME OF YOUR LIFE

Moving In

I am listening
to *The Flying Dutchman,*
that opera of redemption.
I cannot go

anywhere now
without leaving
myself in the snow.
Instead, I tack a poster

to the kitchen wall.
Instead, I hang a curtain
in the shower stall.
Instead, I put the sheets

on the bed.
Instead, I try to remember
what it was you said
before I left.

Instead, I put
the pillowcase
on the pillow.
Instead, I put my shoes

in place on the closet floor
and my underwear
in one dresser drawer,
sweaters in another,

pants on hangars.
Instead, I listen
to *The Flying Dutchman*,
that opera of redemption.

Instead, I put the saucepan
on the nail above
the greasy white
enamel stove.

Instead, I plug in
the electric typewriter
and write trash, write,
trash, hang flypaper.

Instead, I open
the cheap white wine.
Instead, I plug in
the electric typewriter

in a different outlet.
Instead, I hang a calendar.
Instead, I let out my Credo:
I believe in

THE TIME OF YOUR LIFE

this white of snow;
I believe in
this silver of moon;
I believe in

this music of redemption;
I believe in
this green of grass;
I believe in

this believing in less and less.
Here is the telephone,
this terrible instrument,
asleep in its cradle.

Here is the machine-gun
of buttons, loaded weapon
of communication.
Who will be first

to call the other?
Who will be first
to pull the trigger?
Instead, I listen

to *The Flying Dutchman,*
that opera of redemption.
Instead, I write and trash.
Instead, I'm all moved in.

The Simple Past

The simple past is my heaven.
I am preparing for it.

Everyday I remove another bit
of my complexity, like skin, and

toss it in the purifying flame
of time. When I am done, I will be gone.

Except for a stone. And my name.
And my right hand's fingers, burned to bone.

What the Dead Said

The last passion is the passion to last.
This is what they said in my dream. They said,
We saw the future in the mirrored past.

We never believed it could be so fast.
Some sat in chairs. Some stood around the bed.
The last passion is the passion to last.

We never realized it in our haste.
Their voices dropped like stones from drooping heads.
We wanted more than just the mirrored past.

Beneath their feet was empty space, dark, vast,
cold, silent, terrible, terribly sad.
The last passion is the passion to last.

We lived for pleasure, heedless of the waste
until we made the waste of years our need.
We loved the future, and we loathed the past.

Their words were whispered breaths, mere wispy ghosts
of words. Their lips were brass. Their tongues were lead.
We lost the future, and we killed the past.
The last passion is the passion to last.

J.R. Solonche

The Poet From Nepal

The poet from Nepal told us about Nepal,
a poor country, where the people are poor,
and life is hard, but the people there are
happy in spite of being poor, and in spite
of how hard life is in Nepal, and he asked,
What do you teach students in your college
here in your country, do you teach them how
to make money, or do you teach them how
to be happy? and I wanted to answer his
question but I couldn't think of I teach them
that money can't buy happiness, I teach them
how to make just enough money to be happy
and not a penny more, I teach them that
the pursuit of happiness doesn't mean what
they think it does, I teach them that the pursuit
of money doesn't mean what they think it does,
I teach them what Robert Lowell said,
that there is no money in poetry but neither
is there poetry in money, I teach them that
money is the root of all evil and happiness
is for pigs. I couldn't think of all
I wanted to say to the poet from Nepal.

Dog Ghazal

The Saluki is the oldest breed of dog.
Because they were killing his sheep, Jefferson enacted a tax on dogs.

The first animal in space was a dog.
The ancient Chinese kept warm by putting up their sleeves their dogs.

The Basenji is the only barkless dog.
Paul McCartney recorded a high pitched whistle at the end
                              of "A Day in the Life" for his dog.

Sweetlips was the name of George Washington's dog.
Bingo is the name of the Cracker Jacks dog.

Gidget is the name of the Taco Bell dog.
Carlo was the name of Emily Dickinson's dog.

George Lucas modeled the Ewoks after his family dog.
The earth's magnetic field determines the orientation of the
                                      poop of a dog.

    So, Solonche, aren't you going to mention "wagging the dog"
                                                  at all?
    Nope. You can't teach new tricks to an old doggerel.

J.R. Solonche

Undo

You say
it's so simple,
too simple to be true.

Why so suspicious
of simplicity?
Who did this to us?

Was it science?
O, inventor
of complexity,

undo, undo,
I must undo what
you have done.

Because Understanding Ends It Does Not Mean All Ends

Because understanding ends it does not mean all ends.
When understanding goes home, the rest goes on into the unknown.

What happened between us did not happen.
What did not happen between us happened.

We had an understanding.
I do not know what it was we understood.

I'm sure we did not understand each other.
It must have been something between us.

It must have been something halfway between us.
It must have been something just out of your reach between us.

It must have been something just out of my reach between us.
Understanding went home to Blooming Grove.

Understanding went home to Wurtsboro.
The rest went on into the unknown, O, on and on and on, O.

I Don't Believe You Don't Remember

I don't believe you don't remember, for everyone remembers.
You do remember, but you said you don't for a reason.

I don't know what the reason is.
Who is it that you are protecting?

Is it me or is it you that you are protecting?
I told you I remember because I did not want to hurt one of us.

It was because I did not want to hurt you.
Now I think it was because I wanted to hurt myself.

I wanted you to tell me the truth even if to lie.
A lie contains the truth, more than anywhere.

The truth contains all the lies in the world.
The lies are safe there, in the bosom of the truth.

I weep for them, the orphans, the motherless.
I weep for us, who suffer for no reason, for every reason.

Masturbation

Sorry,
my mistake,

I got ahead
of myself.

J.R. Solonche

Autumn

The leaves are gone,
but still not satisfied,
the wind remains,
sighing in the empty
branches of the oaks.

My Lilac is Dying

My lilac is dying.
It's drying and cracking and breaking and dying.
I can hardly smell it anymore.
I used to be able to smell it from the road.
Now I have to get right up next to it to smell it.
Even then the fragrance is thin, so weak and thin.
I cut all the blooms.
I put them into a glass jar.
All the blooms fit into one small glass jar.

J.R. Solonche

Coltsfoot

Spring has slid four days in,
and still winter's cold hand holds on
this icy, cloudy, windy morning.
But look! where yellow wildflowers
have slipped these steely fingers,
have nudged aside dead leaves.
Coltsfoot bristly with yellow rays
in the shallow ditch by the roadside.
New gold buttons on an old overcoat,
a row of coltsfoot in ground-level glory!

The Peacock

The peacock, alone
in the enclosure
with just the flowers,

turns tail and struts off,
displaying only disappointment,
or by now, more likely indifference.

J.R. Solonche

Metamorphosis

Does the monarch butterfly
on the viburnum
know it was not always
a butterfly,
or is it only where memory
ends that wings begin?

You Should Just Let It Go
(very short poem for four voices)

1.
You should.

2.
Just let it.

3.
Go.

4.
Yes, you.

J.R. Solonche

On the Passing of Philip Roth

Philip Roth
is dead.

Just feel
this cloth.

Nine Yellow Lilies

I do not know why
I counted them,
why I had to count
them, the nine
yellow lilies, but
I did count them,
the nine yellow lilies
in my garden. So
if you are a psychologist,
please write to me,
and please explain why
I had to count them,
the nine yellow lilies
in a row in my garden.

J.R. Solonche

The Melancholy of Anatomy

My hand hurts.
It's arthritis.

The pen hurts.
It's a poem.

THE TIME OF YOUR LIFE

The Fun of Poetry

"How can you
read your own
handwriting?"
asks my daughter
flipping through
my notebook.
"Sometimes I can't,"
I reply, "which is
why poetry can
sometimes be fun."

Van Gogh

painted 80 paintings
in the last 70 days
of his life. His last
is "Tree Roots,"
painted the morning
of the day he died.
I want to write 80
poems in the last 70
days of my life.
The last will be
Tree Roots, which
I will write the morning
of the day I die.
I want this because
van Gogh wanted
to be a poet,
because I wanted
to be a painter.

Stargazer Lilies

While carrying the stargazer
lilies to the car,

I got orange stargazer lily
pollen on my shirt.

I gazed at the orange pollen,
promising myself never

to wash the shirt, for here
I was, a nobody, a stranger

who had been touched by a stargazer
that had gazed at a star.

J.R. Solonche

When I Get Up

When I get up
in the morning,
the first thing I do
is look out the window,
not to see if the same
world is still there,
for that is not in doubt.
I do it to see if I still
want to get up and go out
into that same world one more time.

To Each Her Own

On the radio, I heard an interview
with a lady who represents
The International Franchise Association,
and her headstone flashed before my eyes:

So and So,
Beloved Daughter,
Beloved Wife,
Beloved Mother,
Beloved Spokesperson for the International Franchise Association.

J.R. Solonche

Four Short Rosebush Poems

1.
Listen to the red
rosebush.
It is whispering
as loud as it can.

2.
The red rosebush
is surely prolific.
It has made 55 roses.
But they are all red.

THE TIME OF YOUR LIFE

3.
Is the rosebush
this good
at making
red roses
because it has
nothing else to do?

4.
I cannot hold
55 beautiful red
thoughts in
my mind
all at once.
Therefore,
I am not
a rosebush.

J.R. Solonche

Brown Freckles

Last night, playing with her toy crystal ball,
my daughter said,
Dad, tomorrow, you are going to write
a poem called "Brown Freckles."

The Only Thing

The only thing worse
than when nothing
makes sense is when
everything makes sense.

J.R. Solonche

Attraction

The big flowers
attract the big bees,
the little flowers
attract the little bees,
the in between flowers
attract the in between bees.
So it is with poetry.
So it is with poets.

THE TIME OF YOUR LIFE

A Piece of Real Estate

Just.
Where everything
happens,
and nothing, too.

(which is what,
the underbelly
of everything?)
No, not true,

(to really state
the case) *never
nothing,*
never ever that.

There's no
such thing,
only in the mind,
when you

think about it.
What the fuck
do you think
the doves

are doing?
And the flies?
And the birches
back there?

And the clematis
climbing up
the deer fence
and then the air?

Do you think
they're doing
nothing?
Nothing?

Why they're
doing everything,
everything there
is to do.

On the Passing of Clarence Fountain

Sweet Fountain
of Clarence,

I bow down
as you pass.

J.R. Solonche

I Have No Use for the Phrases

I have no use for the phrases,
strange beauty and *mysterious beauty*.

All beauty is strange.
All beauty is mysterious.

Reassurance

"Nothing's humming today," I said.
"Hey, don't complain," said Jim.
"Humming is what you do
when you've forgotten the words."

J.R. Solonche

Poem Beginning with a Line from an Old Chinese Poem

The sun shines on the old garden.
I pick up my chair and open it between
the white peonies and a round stone.

What can be better than sitting down
in an old garden with new flowers in June?
I close my eyes, look that way, become one.

The Breeze

The breeze flips
over the page of
my notebook
lying on the table.
How wiser than I
the breeze is
to know when
the poem should
seal its lips.

J.R. Solonche

Flowers of Guilt

The strawflowers
are dying. From not
enough watering?
From too much watering?
So what good will a poem do them?
Not as much as to my conscience,
withering.

If Days Like This Rare Day

If days like this rare day
are a consolation or a bribe,
if the gods know which it is,
in pity or in jest,
if it is the goddess *Merciful*
or the goddess *Just*
who is responsible,
we cannot say.

J.R. Solonche

Every Place Must

Every place must
have its word,

every word its place,
so what word to put

into place in this place
of brightness of sun,

of softness of breeze,
of distance of death's horizon?

THE TIME OF YOUR LIFE

O, Happy Hour

The rest are not
unhappy hours,
not really, but
ordinary hours,
neither of one kind
nor of another,
sitting there, off by
themselves, minding
their own business,
passing the time
passing the time.

J.R. Solonche

Over the Clouds

Over the clouds
the sun has no control.

They are in control,
the clouds, in their gray line,

not so much a line
as a mass, more than

massive enough to cover
the sun, to own, by force,

almost the sky whole.
Helpless, the sun

grins a gold grin
diminishing,

until it glows out,
goes gray as they

behind them,
finished off finishing.

Wild Cherry Tree in August

The tree as is today
plus my memory
of the tree as was
in April is the tree
I always want to see.

J.R. Solonche

Red Vinca

Stand up straight,
red vinca!
Stand up tall!
You dominate
my garden from
your hanging pots.
You bleed upward
into the sun,
and the weeds
are green with envy.

The Shadows That Shadow Me

1.
Hey, T.S. Eliot,
it doesn't matter
where the shadow falls,
for it falls everywhere.

2.
If the shadow
is too much to bear,
then become it.

3.
Where is
the shadow
of the wind?

4.
The wind
is a shadow,
but of what?

5.
There can
never be
too many
shadows.

6.
The night
is nothing
more than
a shadow.

7.
In shadow,
where do
colors go?

8.
Nothing
is more
shallow
than shadow.

9.
What you
remember
of this poem
is its shadow.

10.
What is light
if not the shadow
of shadow?

THE TIME OF YOUR LIFE

The Old Rosebush

I thought the rosebush was dead
just like the other rose bushes were dead.
In fact, I wanted the rosebush
to be dead just like the other rosebushes
were dead. But, lo, out of spite,
and behold, it made a rose!

J.R. Solonche

The Mushrooms

The mushrooms
must make room
for themselves
at the base
of the oak tree
which does not
begrudge it,
unless, as more
likely, it doesn't know.

The Acorns

The acorns
are falling
and it's only
August. Isn't
it too soon?
Ah, only
in a poem,
one like this,
can we pretend
that all is fine,
that nothing,
nothing is amiss.

J.R. Solonche

The Hummingbird at the Empty Feeder

stops at every station
and finding nothing,
moves on.
This is a lesson,
all right, but listen,
I'm not that kind of poet,
and this is not that kind of hummingbird.

Metaphor

There's a crack
in my glass
of bourbon
on the rocks,
and I don't
give a shit
what it means
as long as
it doesn't leak.

J.R. Solonche

The Next Time

The next time I see the word *Kafkaesque*,
I'm going to puke.
He wasn't put on trial for anything.
His life was his trial.
He wasn't guilty of anything.
His life was his guilt.
It was the Abraham and Isaac story without Abraham.
Or with Yahweh playing both the fathers.
In the end, Isaac sacrifices himself.

The Nowhere

The nowhere
to be found

is not the same
nowhere

as the nowhere
to be seen.

J.R. Solonche

Petunias

They should have died
a dozen deaths by now,
but here they are,
alive as ever,
as when we planted
them three months ago,
none the worse for wear,
for being worn down.
What chins they must
have taking the sun,
taking the rain, as
they have taken,
as we have taken
them for granted.
Let us praise petunias!
Let us raise our glasses
to petunias! Petunias!

THE TIME OF YOUR LIFE

I Am Waiting for Something

I am waiting for something.
It is for the day,
for the moment of the day,
when I will say,
"I am not waiting anymore,
for there is nothing more
worth waiting for."

J.R. Solonche

Summer

Summer is nearly done,
fall almost begun.
I know because I hear
the birds talking among
themselves and the insects
whisper, with shriller wings,
their warnings.

THE TIME OF YOUR LIFE

One Is Forced to Admire It

One is forced to admire it,
this tiny tuft of grass
forcing its way, (yes,
forcing with all its might!)
up between the paving stones,
knowing it will get nowhere,
yet just as near the sun
as the top of that fir tree
way up there.

J.R. Solonche

In the Depth at the Height of Summer

In the depth at the height of the summer,
the trees are as gold as green,
and the sky is as gold as blue,
and the clouds are as gold as white,
and I am as gold as I'll ever be,
which is to say,
gold as rust.

The Music

The music is never irrelevant, never.
It is always the only way to travel, here or there.

Without music, the silence would be too much to bear.
Without music, the science would be too much to bear.

I want to die to music.
I want death to sing to blues guitar acoustic.

The physicists say the universe hums its own unaccompanied music.
If we had ears the size of galaxies, we could hear it.

When I die, my ears will be galaxies.
When I die, I will hear the universe hum its own unaccompanied music.

I will never forgive the gods for denying me a life in music.
Gods, with your ears of galaxies, do you hear?

I would rather sing in Carnegie Hall once than write 1000 poems.
Death, do you hear me? (Sigh.)

I want you to set these words to blues guitar acoustic.
I tell you, if there is no music after death, I will die.

Acknowledgments

THE MILO REVIEW
"On a Picture Entitled Jesus at Twelve Years of Age"

OFFCOURSE LITERARY JOURNAL
"April"
"Finding a Flower Pressed between Pages of the 1887 Edition of *The Early Poems of John Greenleaf Whittier*"

RIGHT HAND POINTING
"Summer"

STREETLIGHT
"I Bought Them"

CHRONOGRAM
"Second Warning to a Young Poet"

About the Author

Professor Emeritus of English at SUNY Orange, **J.R. Solonche** has been publishing poetry in magazines, journals, and anthologies since the early 70s. Notable among these are *The American Scholar, The New Criterion, The Progressive, The Journal of the American Medical Association, Poetry Northwest, The North American Review, Poetry East, The Literary Review, The Hampden-Sydney Poetry Review, The American Journal of Poetry, Salmagundi, Hawaii Pacific Review*, and *Poet Lore*, as well as the anthologies *Visiting Frost, A Ritual to Read Together: Poems in Conversation with William Stafford, Mixed Voices: Contemporary Poems about Music, Facing the Change: Personal Encounters with Global Warming, Dogs Singing: A Tribute Anthology, Beyond Lament: Poets of the World Bearing Witness to the Holocaust,* and the *Anthology of Magazine Verse & Yearbook of American Poetry.* He is the author of **Beautiful Day** (Deerbrook Editions), **Won't Be Long** (Deerbrook Editions), **Heart's Content** (Five Oaks Press), **Invisible** (nominated for the Pulitzer Prize by Five Oaks Press), **The Black Birch** (Kelsay Books), **I, Emily Dickinson & Other Found Poems** (Deerbrook Editions), **In Short Order** (Kelsay Books), **Tomorrow, Today and Yesterday** (Deerbrook Editions), **True Enough** (Dos Madres Press), **The Jewish Dancing Master** (Ravenna Press), **If You Should See Me Walking on the Road** (Kelsay Books), **In a Public Place** (Dos Madres Press), **To Say the Least** (Dos Madres Press), **For All I Know** (Kelsay Books), **The Porch Poems** (Deerbrook Editions), **Enjoy Yourself** (Serving House Books), and coauthor of **Peach Girl: Poems for a Chinese Daughter** (Grayson Books). He lives in the Hudson Valley.

www.ingramcontent.com/pod-product-compliance
Lightning Source LLC
Chambersburg PA
CBHW032237080426
42735CB00008B/893